curious about
EARTHQUAKES
I0813494
BY RACHEL GRACK
AMICUS LEARNING

What are you

curious about?

Curious About is published by
Amicus Learning, an imprint of Amicus
P.O. Box 227, Mankato, MN 56002
www.amicuspublishing.us

Editor: Ana Brauer
Series Designer: Kathleen Petelinsek
Book Designer and Photo Researcher: Kathleen Petelinsek

Library of Congress Cataloging-in-Publication Data
Names: Koestler-Grack, Rachel A., 1973– author
Title: Curious about earthquakes / by Rachel Grack.
Description: Mankato, MN : Amicus Learning, an imprint of Amicus [2026] | Series: Curious about extreme weather | Includes bibliographical references and index. | Audience: Ages 6–9 | Audience: Grades 2–3 | Summary: "Where do earthquakes happen? Learn the causes and effects of one of nature's most unpredictable events in this question-and-answer book for elementary-aged readers. Includes infographics, table of contents, glossary, books and websites for further research, and index"— Provided by publisher.
Identifiers: LCCN 2025011920 (print) | LCCN 2025011921 (ebook) | ISBN 9798892008372 library binding | ISBN 9798892009034 paperback | ISBN 9798892009690 ebook
Subjects: LCSH: Earthquakes—Juvenile literature
Classification: LCC QE521.3 .K636 2026 (print) | LCC QE521.3 (ebook) | DDC 551.22—dc23/eng/20250717
LC record available at https://lccn.loc.gov/2025011920
LC ebook record available at https://lccn.loc.gov/2025011921

Photo Credits: Alamy Stock Photo/Diarmuid, cover, 1; Shutterstock/dkroy, 12–13, Fly_and_Dive, 16–17, imdproduction, 22, 23, maroke, 21, menur, 13, Naeblys, 10–11, New Africa, 20, NigelSpiers, 5, Ningaloo.gg, 6–7, obert paul van beets, 2, 8, Tartila, 9, VectorMine, 11; Wikimedia Commons/Idaho National Laboratory, 3, 19, Pierre St. Amand, 14, public domain, 2, 14, U.S. Navy photo by Photographer's Mate 2nd Class Philip A. McDaniel, 15, Victor Morozov, 15, 岩手県宮古市, 15

CHAPTER ONE

What are earthquakes?

Boom! You hear a low rumble. The ground suddenly starts shaking. It rocks the whole house. The floor rattles under your feet. It twists and knocks you down. Furniture tips over. Windows pop and walls crack. An earthquake has struck. It is a scary surprise.

Earthquakes are also called shocks.

DID YOU KNOW?

An earthquake makes noise. It sounds like rolling thunder, a loud boom, or a rushing train.

Where do earthquakes happen?

DID YOU KNOW?
Long fault lines cause the strongest shocks.

Most take place along major **fault** lines. These are cracks in the Earth's surface. The most famous is the San Andreas Fault in California. It is also the longest. But there are countless faults all over the world. Any of them could cause an earthquake.

The San Andreas Fault in California is about 800 miles (1,300 kilometers) long.

Strong shocks can destroy buildings.

How often do earthquakes take place?

Hundreds happen every day. Most are too small to feel. The size is measured in **magnitude**. Scientists rate them from one to 10 on the Richter Scale. Strong shocks take place almost every month. Great earthquakes happen about once a year.

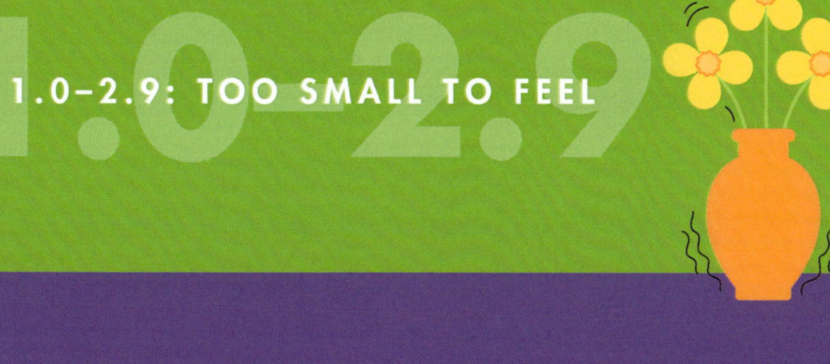

1.0–2.9: TOO SMALL TO FEEL

3.0–4.9: LIGHT

5.0–6.9: SOMEWHAT STRONG

7.0–7.9: STRONG

8.0+: GREAT

RICHTER SCALE

CHAPTER TWO

What causes an earthquake?

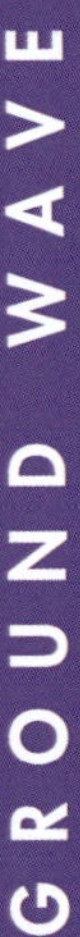

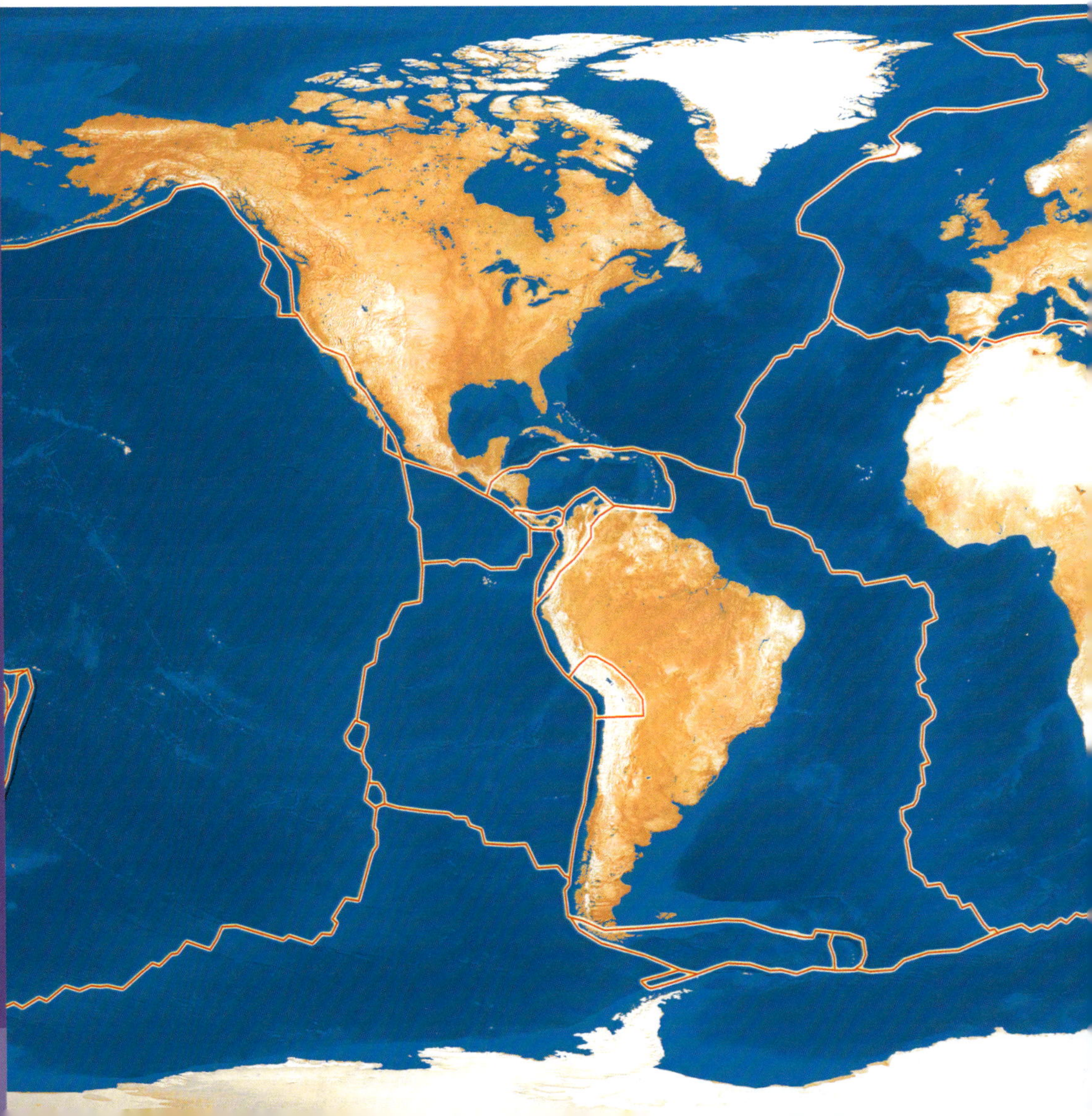

The Earth's crust is made of huge **tectonic plates**. The pieces slowly move around. Sometimes they get stuck. Then they suddenly slip past each other. The shock sends out **seismic waves**. They shake the ground. Some can be felt hundreds of miles (kilometers) away.

Earthquakes can happen when tectonic plates move in different directions.

A seismograph in California records the earth's movement.

How do you know when one happens?

The lines on a seismograph go from smooth to jagged during an earthquake.

Zigzags show up on a seismograph. This machine records movement in the earth. It is firmly mounted on the ground. A heavy weight hangs on a spring from the frame. It bounces when the earth shakes. A pen draws the movement on a spinning roll of paper.

What was the worst earthquake?

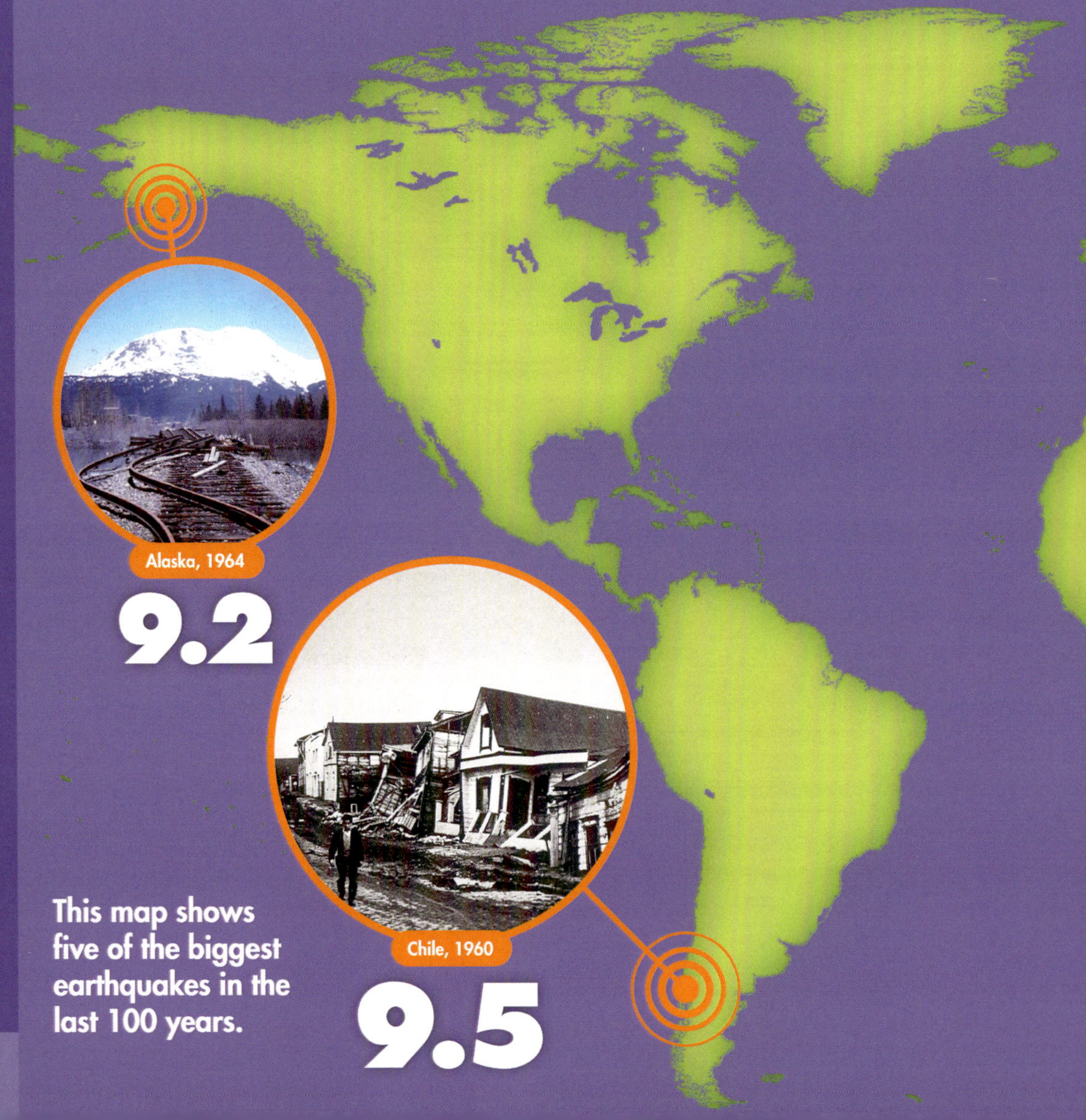

This map shows five of the biggest earthquakes in the last 100 years.

That took place in China in 1556. It shook more than 97 countries. Mountains fell apart. The ground ripped wide open. It caused fires and **landslides**. Rivers changed course and flooded over. Whole villages were buried under piles of rock. About 830,000 people died.

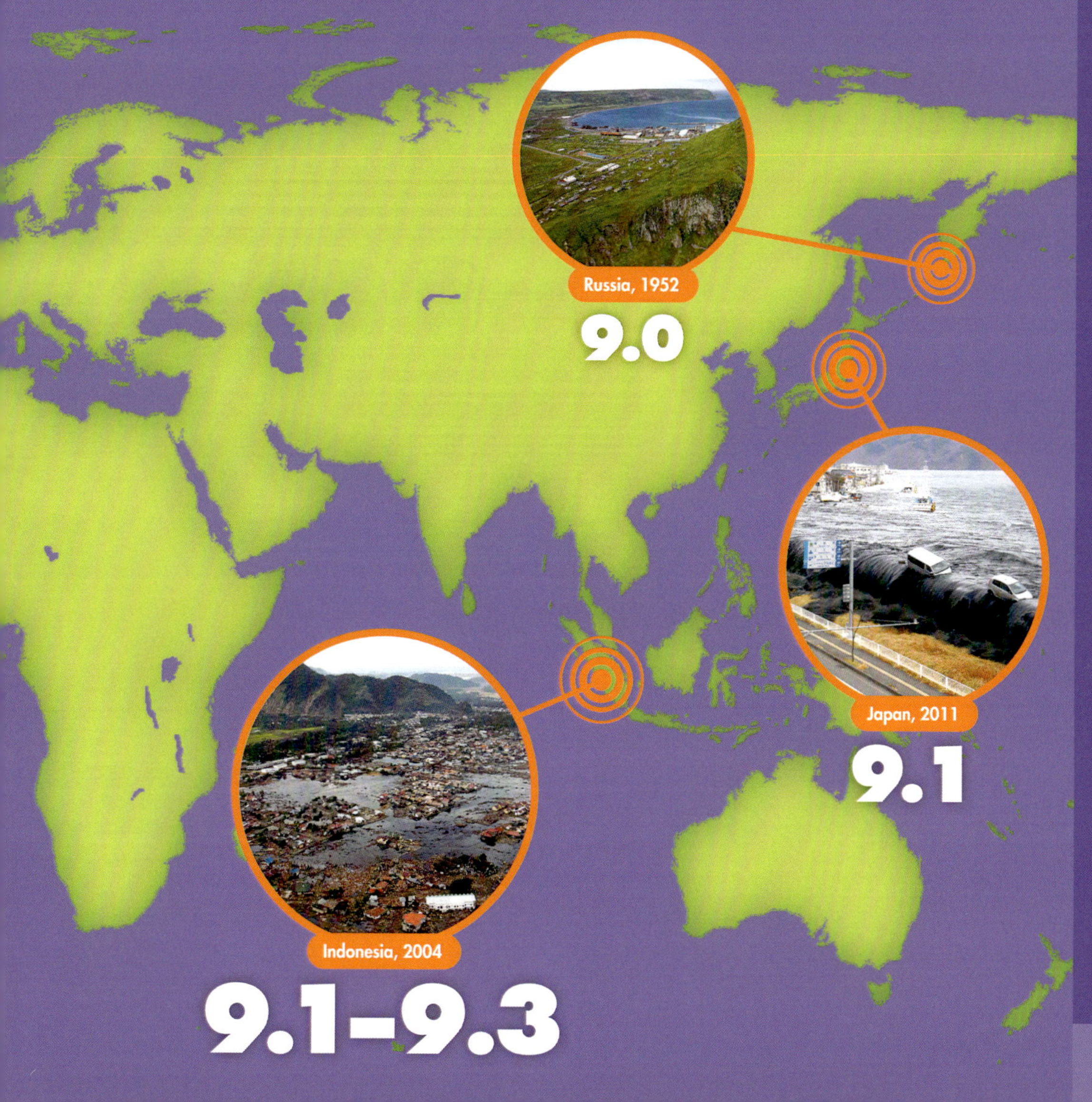

Why are earthquakes so deadly?

DID YOU KNOW?
Houses can be built to better withstand an earthquake. Builders use materials that add strength and allow movement.

A tsunami caused a lot of damage in Fukushima, Japan, in 2011.

People have little time to act before it's too late. Other wild weather quickly follows. Earthquakes cause floods, mudslides, and avalanches. Some rock the ocean floor and start **tsunamis**. These huge walls of water crash ashore. They wipe out whole cities within minutes.

CHAPTER THREE

Do we know when earthquakes will strike?

Sadly, no. We know where they are most likely to happen. Seismic stations measure ground movement near these spots. Scientists warn people as soon as possible. Sometimes a light **foreshock** comes first. But not always. **Aftershocks** follow most earthquakes, though. They can continue for weeks, months, or even years.

DID YOU KNOW?

There are more than 150 seismic recording stations around the world.

A seismic station helps scientists watch for earthquakes in Idaho.

What should I do if I feel one?

You can make an emergency kit to be ready for earthquakes.

Crawl under a heavy table or bed. Cover your head with your arms. Hold onto whatever you are underneath. Move with it if it starts to slide. No furniture nearby? Kneel next to a wall away from a window. Wait there until the shaking stops.

DID YOU KNOW?
Shocks often destroy whole cities. Help your community clean up and rebuild as soon as it is safe.

It is important to know what to do in the event of an earthquake.

ASK MORE QUESTIONS

Do I live near a fault line?

Which country has the most earthquakes?

Try a BIG QUESTION: Where is the safest place in my house during an earthquake?

SEARCH FOR ANSWERS

Search the library catalog or the Internet.
A librarian, teacher, or parent can help you.

Using Keywords
Find the looking glass.

Keywords are the most important words in your question.

?

If you want to know about:

- to see nearby fault lines, type: FAULT LINES NEAR (YOUR CITY)
- to find out where most earthquakes happen, type: COUNTRIES WITH MOST EARTHQUAKES

FIND GOOD SOURCES

Here are some good, safe sources you can use in your research.
Your librarian can help you find more.

Books

Earthquakes
by Marcia Abramson, 2023.

Earthquakes and the Environment
by Jamee-Marie Edwards, 2025.

Internet Sites

National Geographic Kids: Earthquake
https://kids.nationalgeographic.com/science/article/earthquake
National Geographic Kids is an educational website for kids.

Weather Wiz Kids: Earthquakes
https://www.weatherwizkids.com/weather-earthquake.htm
Weather Wiz Kids is an educational website about weather for kids. Learn about all kinds of weather!

Every effort has been made to ensure that these websites are appropriate for children. However, because of the nature of the Internet, it's impossible to guarantee that these sites will remain active indefinitely or that their contents will not be altered.

SHARE AND TAKE ACTION

Build two towers on a cookie sheet—one with wooden blocks and one with LEGO bricks.
Shake the cookie sheet. What happens to each tower? Talk about ways to build structures to withstand earthquakes.

Build your own seismograph with simple supplies.
Ask an adult to help you search the internet for ideas.

Practice an earthquake drill with friends.
Who picked the safest spot?

GLOSSARY

aftershock A smaller earthquake that takes place after a large one.

fault The cracks in the Earth's crust where tectonic plates meet.

foreshock A light earthquake that happens just before a stronger one in the same spot.

landslide Masses of earth and trees that slide down a mountainside.

magnitude The strength of something.

seismic wave A wave of energy formed by an earthquake.

tectonic plate A large, flat piece of Earth's surface that slowly moves.

tsunami An unusually large sea wave produced by an earthquake or volcanic eruption.

INDEX

About the Author

Rachel Grack has been editing and writing children's books since 1999. She lives on a small ranch in the Arizona desert.